MAKING SENSE OF GOD IN THIS CHAOTIC WORLD

(No Plan B)

by

James Hammond and Joseph Hammond

DORRANCE PUBLISHING CO
EST. 1920
PITTSBURGH, PENNSYLVANIA 15238

All quotations are from the King James Bible unless noted otherwise. References are taken from BibleSoft, PC Study Bible Version 5

Dorrance Publishing Co
585 Alpha Drive
Suite 103
Pittsburgh, PA 15238
Visit our website at www.dorrancebookstore.com

ISBN: 978-1-4809-8701-2
eISBN: 978-1-4809-8724-1

We'd like to dedicate this book to:

Joe and Victoria Bisconti
And
Deborah Hammond

Thank you for all your help!

INTRODUCTION

As Christians, what can we know about God? What are His characteristics? Does He love or hate? Is He grieved by anything? Does He have expectations about his creation? If He does, are those expectations reasonable? How does He differ from us, and how is He the same? Why do sickness, and death, and poverty, and lack exist in a world He created? Did He create it to be that way? Is putting sickness or disease on us His way of teaching us a lesson? Some people think so, but what kind of God would do that? Is God willing to communicate with us, and if so, how would He do it? Does God care if I'm tired, or hungry, or destitute, or alone and unloved? Can He sympathize with my plight in this life? Has He taken any action at all to make my life better here? I mean, He created us, so why is there so much chaos in the world?

WHERE DO WE STAND IN CHRIST?

God is Love.

For He so loved the world that He gave. God is a giver beyond comprehension: He loved us all, even when we were living in the darkness of sin. When the first man, Adam, sinned, instead of destroying all of His creation and beginning over again, the Father offered up His only son, Jesus, as a sacrifice for the sins of all in order to set us free (John 3:16). Only someone without the taint of sin could pay the price for the sin of all humanity; and Jesus, the Word of God made flesh, willingly offered Himself as that sacrifice out of love. *...Who for the joy that was set before him, endured the cross, despising the shame, and is set down at the right hand of the throne of God* (Heb 12:2). Desiring peace for us and not evil, He planned for us to have a real hope and a future (Jer. 29:11). God is good, so good!

Jas. 1:17. *Every good gift and every perfect gift is from above and cometh down from the Father of lights, with whom there is no variableness neither shadow of turning* (He does not change).

John 10:10. *The thief cometh not but for to steal, and to kill, and to destroy: I (Jesus) am come that they might have life and that they might have it more abundantly.*

11. *I am the good shepherd: the good shepherd gives his life for the sheep.*

God is good…so very good! That's who He is! Every action He takes is grounded by love, even the hard things.

However, the thief (Satan) comes to steal, kill, and destroy; and bringing darkness into our lives gives him great pleasure because he hates everything that God created. He is called the "god" of this world in 2 Cor. 4:4, because, though God gave complete dominion of the Earth to Adam, when Adam sinned, his connection with God was broken and he became a slave to Satan, who then assumed his authority. Satan stole that authority through deception, yet it is a valid authority nevertheless. His authority will remain until Adam's lease runs out. So much of what people blame God for is not really done by Him at all. God has to allow many things to happen because of Adam's defection and Satan's dominion and legal rights. This is a fallen world we live in. God has to have one of "His" people "ask" Him to do something before He can even intervene in a situation; because other than Satan and his minions, only a human being on the Earth who is an heir and joint heir with Christ has authority here (Rom. 8:17). Jesus' death and His blood paid the price for our sin and re-established our rights of dominion on this Earth. Everything that sin took away (resulting in poverty, sickness, disease, lack, lost dominion, and death) was re-established by Jesus' death at Calvary, although a cessation of physical death will actually take place at a future date.

It's interesting that the Greek word for "ask" is a command in many instances such as: John.14:13; John. 15:7; James.1:5, and it is really "a demand for something due." Therefore John 14:13, 14 would read: *And whatsoever ye shall demand as something due in my name, that will I do, that the Father may be glorified in the Son. If you demand anything in my name, I will do it.*

We can come boldly before the throne of God and respectfully demand the legal rights that Jesus obtained for us, and Satan can't prevent our getting it, because it's based on God's Word. We must know and understand His Word and absolutely believe it, because that's how we plead our case with Him. It is a legal system, and it would be wise of us to understand our legal rights with God and operate in them. Sure, God knows all things. He knows what's going on in your life, but He must be asked before He can step into your situation.

On that positive note, those who are born again in Christ are now citizens of the Kingdom of Heaven and are not under Satan's authority at all. For us, Satan is a defeated foe: Jesus made an open show of him before all of heaven (Col. 2:15) when He rose from the dead with the keys to death and hell. Through Jesus we are kings and priests (Rev. 1:6) and we are to "reign in life" by one Jesus Christ (Rom. 5:17). It is our privilege as citizens of heaven to bring the good news of salvation to a dying world.

Matt. 28:19. *Go ye therefore, and teach all nations, baptizing them in the name of the Father, and of the Son, and of the Holy Ghost: teaching them to observe all things whatsoever I have commanded you: and lo, I am with you always, even unto the end of the world. Amen.*

Mark 16:17. *And these signs shall follow them that believe: in my name they shall cast out devils; they shall speak with mew tongues;*

18. *They shall take up serpents* (if they are bitten by a serpent, it shall not harm them); *and if they drink any deadly thing, it shall not hurt them; they shall lay hands on the sick, and they shall recover.* (He put all that in there so that none of Satan's attempts to destroy us as Jesus' personal ambassadors would succeed. When the Apostle Paul was shipwrecked on the Island of Melita, while gathering wood for a fire, a viper fastened to his hand, and the natives who watched expected him to die quickly. Instead of dying, Paul simply shook off the viper into the fire and went about his business, unharmed [Acts 28:3]. We have that same protection.)

We were born into this fallen world with a missing ingredient: something that we have to find and accept before we can be complete in the way God intended us to be. That something is the presence of God himself in our spirit. When we accept Jesus as Lord and Savior because He paid the price for our sin, we finally feel and know in our hearts that this is what we have always wanted and needed. There is a peace in our lives that defies comprehension, and our hearts overflow with joy. Yes, there are many blessings to being a child of God, but the greatest blessing is to enjoy a loving relationship with God our Father. *But seek ye first the kingdom of God and his righteousness, and all these things shall be added unto you* (Matt. 6:33). We have to make our relationship with the Father the most important thing in our lives, and we can't let anything come before that or push it out of the way. Our eternity hinges on that.

We are Righteous

Rom. 5:17-19. *17. For if by one man's offence death reigned by one; much more they which receive <u>abundance of grace</u> and the <u>gift of righteousness</u> shall reign in life by one Jesus Christ.*

18. Therefore as by the offence of one, judgment came upon all men to condemnation, even so by the righteousness of one, the free gift (righteousness) *came upon all men unto justification of life.*

19. For as by one man's (Adam's) *disobedience many were made sinners, so by the obedience of one* (Jesus) *shall many be made righteous.*

2 Cor. 5:21. *For he hath made him* (Jesus) *to be sin for us, who knew no sin; that we might be made the <u>righteousness</u> of God in him.* (This great exchange is made the moment we are born again, made new in Christ)

1 John 2:29. *If ye know that he* (Jesus) *is righteous, you know that everyone that doeth righteousness is born of him.*

1 John 3:7. *Little children, let no man deceive you, he that doeth righteousness is <u>righteous</u>* (in right standing with God), *even as He is righteous.*

As you can see from these scriptures, righteousness with God is a free gift to us, not because we earned it, but because of God's grace and His unmerited favor. That favor gives us the power both to desire and to perform what God asks of us.

The Sin Problem

1 John 1:8. *If we say that we have no sin, we deceive ourselves, and the truth is not in us.*

If we confess our sins, He is faithful and just to forgive us our sins and to cleanse us from all unrighteousness.

If we say that we have not sinned, we make Him a liar, and His word is not in us.

Rom. 10:9. *That if thou shall confess with thy mouth the Lord Jesus, and shall believe with thine heart that God hath raised him from the dead, thou shall be saved.*

For with the heart man believeth unto righteousness, and <u>with the mouth confession is made unto salvation.</u>

(Representing our dying—the old man of sin—with Christ, and our burial with Him in the grave, we are a part of His resurrection from the dead and are now seated with Him in heavenly places: That's what baptism signifies. However, baptism means nothing if we don't first recognize in our hearts that we are sinners who need a savior. Repenting of that sin and fully accepting that Jesus, who came in the flesh as man, really was God, we also acknowledge that He died for our sins on the cross and completed the transaction when He rose from the dead. We then confess Him to be our Lord and Savior <u>with our mouth</u>; for with the heart we believe unto right standing with God, but with the mouth we confess unto salvation. There are those who believe that, because they are church members and are baptized, that they are saved; but baptism has nothing to do with salvation.)

It's important to realize what actually takes place in the salvation experience. In the beginning God created us in His own image:

Gen. 1:26. *And God said, let us make man in our own image, after our likeness, and let them have dominion over the fish of the sea, and over the fowl of the air, and over the cattle, and over all the earth, and over every creeping thing that creeps over the earth.*

Well, what is God's likeness, His image? The Gospel of John tells us:

John 4:24. *God is a Spirit and they that worship him must worship in spirit and in truth.*

So God is a Spirit. Do we have a spirit?

1 Thess. 5:23. *And the very God of peace sanctify you wholly; and I pray God your whole spirit, soul, and body be preserved blameless unto the coming of our Lord Jesus Christ.*

So Paul tells us in 1 Thessalonians that we have a spirit, a soul, and a body. Spirit and soul is not the same thing: There are two different Greek words used for them. The soul of a man is the mind, will, and emotions, and Romans 12:1-2 gives instruction about "our" responsibility for both the soul and body:

Rom 12:1-2. *I beseech you therefore brethren, by the mercies of God, that ye present your bodies a living sacrifice, holy, acceptable to God, which is your reasonable service.*

And be not conformed to this world, but be ye transformed by the renewing of your mind, that ye may prove what is that good, acceptable, and perfect will of God.

The soul is linked to the spirit and the body, but the body is linked only to the soul, not to the spirit. Whichever pair is linked together, either the soul siding with the spirit, or the soul siding with the body, determines how you will walk with the Lord: in the Spirit or in the flesh (soul and body). If you'll notice, we are the ones who are required to present our bodies as a living sacrifice, not God. That's our part and a living sacrifice doesn't like to remain on the altar: It requires a lot of monitoring.

In the second verse, "be not conformed" and "be transformed" are imperative verbs, which means they are commands from God, not just suggestions. We are commanded to be transformed by renewing our minds with the word of God and to not be conformed to this world. Failure to do so leaves us unable to truly discern God's plan and will for our lives, and severely handicaps our walk with the Lord. Most people ignore that admonition, never searching the Word for themselves to see what's really true and what's not. But Paul had praise for those of the church in Berea because they were faithful to check the Word to be sure it was sound teaching (Acts 17:10-12).

2 Ti 2:15 (NKJV). *Be diligent to present yourself approved to God, a worker who does not need to be ashamed, rightly dividing the word of truth.*

Ultimately, we are responsible for our own spiritual condition before God. God does want you to prosper and be in health, even as your soul prospers (3 John 1:2), and your soul can only prosper if it is renewed with the Word of God. Through that renewal, God's goal for you is to conform to the image of His son, Jesus.

Rom. 8:29. *For whom he did foreknow, he also did predestinate to be conformed into the image of his son, that he might be the firstborn of many brethren.*

2 Cor. 3:18. *But we all, with open face beholding as in a glass the glory of the Lord, are changed into the same image from glory to glory, even as by the Spirit of the Lord.*

Rom 7:22 Amp. *For I endorse and delight in the law of God in my inmost self* (with my new nature).

23. *But I discern in my bodily members (in the sensitive appetites and will of the flesh) a different law (rule of action) at war against the law of my mind (my reason) and making me a prisoner to the law of sin that dwells in my bodily organs (in the sensitive appetites and will of the flesh).*

24. *O unhappy and pitiable and wretched man that I am! Who will release and deliver me from (the shackles of) this body of death?*

25. *O thank God! (He will!) Through Jesus Christ (the Anointed one) our Lord. So then indeed I, of myself with the heart and mind, serve the law of God, but with the flesh the law of sin.*

There again, if the soul with the spirit serves God's law, then we will not follow the flesh and serve sin. There is a reason for transforming your mind with the word: We are three-part beings comprised of spirit, soul, and body. If the soul retains little knowledge of God's word, then the soul will readily join with the body in living a sinful life; but if the soul is transformed with a strong knowledge of the word and a desire to please God, it will join with the spirit and cut short those thoughts that Satan attacks the mind with, and cooperate with the spirit in living a pure life. (Your mind is the battlefield where Satan attacks.) Whatever you meditate on is what you will do. So if you are continually confessing that you are a sinner (which is what the enemy says about you, not God) you are allowing the enemy access to your mind with thoughts that you don't need to entertain. By thinking continually about things that are not acceptable to God's word, we conceive sin in our minds and then naturally give birth to it. It's almost impossible to abort it once you've spent time meditating on it and desiring it.

Jas. 1:14-15. *But every man is tempted, when he is drawn away of his own lust, and enticed.*

15. *Then when lust hath conceived* (in the mind), *it bringeth forth sin: and sin, when it is finished, bringeth forth death.*

When you confess righteousness (which is yours by the Word of God as a free gift) that's what you will meditate on and maintain in your life. It's pretty simple, really. God also gives an abundance of grace to help in time of need (Rom. 5:17) so that we can withstand temptation; but the bottom line is that our words, our confession, must line up with God's Word in order to live God's kind of life and we must be fully committed to Him. When we step out in God's Word and judge Him faithful, that's when the Word comes alive and becomes our reality.

2 Co. 10:5. *Casting down imaginations and every high thing that exalts itself against the knowledge of God, and bringing into captivity every thought to the obedience of Christ.*

You'll have a difficult time bringing every thought into captivity if your knowledge of the word is lacking. We renew our minds by reprogramming it to the word of God. Until we are born-again, our minds are conformed to Satan's world-view, and that view is enmity with God, utterly opposed to Him. Until then we operate only out of our natural mind, and the natural mind can't understand spiritual things.

Joshua.1:8-9. *8. This book of the law shall not depart out of thy mouth* (the Complete Jewish Bible translates it: *Yes, keep this book of the Torah on your lips*); *but thou shall <u>meditate</u> therein day and night, that thou may observe to do all that is written therein: for then thou shall make thy way prosperous, and then thou shall have good success.*

9. Have I not commanded thee? Be strong and of a good courage, be not afraid, neither be thou dismayed: for the Lord thy God is with thee whithersoever thy go.

<u>We have a better covenant founded upon better promises</u>, but the method for our prospering is still the same: The Word of God must not depart from our mouth. We keep it on our lips, for it is always ready to be spoken, and we say about ourselves what God says about us in that Word. We meditate on it day and night, for then we shall make our way prosperous, and then we shall have good success. If I confess that I have abundance of grace, that I am made righteous, and that I reign in life by one Jesus Christ (Rom. 5:17), I am telling the truth, no matter how I feel about it, because God tells me in His Word that this is who I am as a born-again believer. It would pay to look at all the verses in the New Testament that unfold your relationship with Christ: Those are promises for you.

Spirit of a Man

Hebrews 4:12. *For the Word of God is quick and powerful and sharper than any two-edged sword, piercing even to the dividing asunder of soul and spirit, and of the joints and marrow, and is a discerner of the thoughts and intents of the heart.*

I think it's interesting that the Word of God divides asunder between soul and spirit, because that's exactly what takes place when the spirit is created new within us. Splitting apart the strong bond between the soul and the old spirit with its sinful nature (the old man), God replaces it with a new spirit having His sinless nature. When Adam sinned, it was his spirit within that died to God's life, and we all inherited that loss. Now, when we accept what Jesus did for us and acknowledge his Lordship, our spirit is recreated within us, opening the lines of communication between us and God.

Just as the dividing asunder between soul and spirit provides regeneration of the spiritual part of us, the dividing between joints and marrow by the Word of God provides an example of the physical healing of the body, which is available to all by Christ's death and resurrection. In this situation, things like leukemia and bone cancer and a multitude of other disorders are healed by the Word of God dividing between the bone and marrow and doing a work of eliminating the harmful cells and healing, strengthening, and rejuvenating all that was affected.

Yes, the Word of God is a discerner of the thoughts and intents of the heart. Reading or hearing that Word brings reproof, correction, and instruction in righteousness (1 Tim. 3:16), and all of this happens because God's Word is powerful. The Father spoke that Word into being, investing it with His power, and then when we speak His Word, that power is released into our situation here.

1 John 3:8. *He that commits sin is of the devil, for the devil sinned from the beginning. For this purpose the Son of God was manifested, that he might destroy the works of the devil.*

9. *Whoever is born of God does not commit sin, for his seed remains in him, and he cannot sin, because he is born of God.*

Here John is talking about the "spirit" of a man, not the body and soul. Because God's seed is within us as born-again believers, our spirit within us cannot sin. It remains pure and holy and is the temple of the Holy Spirit.

2 Co. 1:22. *Who hath also sealed us, and given us the earnest of the Spirit in our hearts.*

2 Co. 1:22 Amplified. *(He has also appropriated and acknowledged us as his by) putting his seal upon us and giving us his (Holy) Spirit in our hearts as the security deposit and guarantee (of the fulfillment of his promise).*

Dead to Sin

Rom. 6:6. *Knowing this, that our old man is crucified with him, that the body of sin* (sin nature) *might be destroyed, and that henceforth we should not serve sin.*

7. For he that is dead is free from sin.

Rom 7:4. *Wherefore, my brethren, ye are also become dead to the law by the body of Christ, that ye should be married to another* (Jesus), *even to him who is raised from the dead, that ye should bring forth fruit unto God.*

Rom. 6:11. *Likewise reckon ye also yourselves to be dead unto sin, but alive unto God through Jesus Christ our Lord.*

12. Let not sin therefore reign in your mortal body, that you should obey it in the lust thereof.

13. For sin shall not have dominion over you: for ye are not under the law, but under grace.

Rom 4:15. *Because the law works wrath: for where no law is, there is no transgression* (no sin).

Rom 6:15. *What then? Shall we sin because we are not under the law, but under grace? God forbid.*

Know ye not, that to whom ye yield yourselves to obey, <u>his servants ye are to whom ye obey; whether of sin unto death, or of obedience unto righteousness.</u>

But God be thanked, that ye were the servants of sin, but <u>ye obeyed</u> from the heart that form of doctrine that was delivered unto you.

Being then made free from sin, ye became the servants of righteousness.

For when ye were the servants to sin, ye were free from righteousness.

But now, being made free from sin, and become servants to God, ye have your fruit unto holiness, and the end everlasting life.

Even the Apostles, before salvation became an accomplished fact, were declared clean by Jesus:

John 15:3. *Now you are clean through the word I have spoken to you.*

This word "clean" means: pure, clean, innocent, and undefiled, in the Exegetical Dictionary. They were made pure by hearing and believing the words of Jesus before salvation became an actual reality. It became reality when Jesus rose from the dead and presented His blood on the mercy seat before the throne in heaven (Hebrews 9:11-12).

1 John 3:2. *Beloved, now are we the sons of God, and it doth not appear what we shall be: but we know that, when he shall appear, we shall be like him; for we shall see him as he is.*

3. *And every man that hath this hope in him <u>purifyeth himself</u>, even as he is pure.*

Acts 15:9. *And made no distinction between us and them, <u>purifying their hearts</u> by faith.*

Acts 26:18. *...that they may receive forgiveness of sins, and an inheritance among those who are <u>sanctified</u> by faith in me* (Jesus).

Eph 5:25-26. 25. *...Christ also loved the church, and gave himself for it;*

26. *That he might <u>cleanse it</u> with the washing of water by the Word.*

From the moment that we are born of God, we are being cleansed continually by the Word of God, by the hope and faith we have in that Word.

So the old man was crucified with Christ that the body of sin, the sin nature, might be destroyed, and now we are joined with Christ that we may bring forth fruit unto God. We are alive in Him! Yet it is our own free will which decides whether to yield to what He has done for us, or to continue serving sin and reaping death in our lives. Sin shall no longer have dominion over us, but only if we cooperate with God and his overcoming grace. The path we take and the dedication we have to the Lord is still a matter of our choice.

Matt. 7:24. *Therefore whoever heareth these sayings of mine, and doeth them, I will liken him to a wise man, which built his house upon a rock.*

25. *And the rain descended, and the flood came, and the winds blew and beat upon that house; and it fell not: for it was founded upon a rock.*

26. *And every one that heareth these sayings of mine, and doeth them not, shall be likened unto a foolish man, which built his house upon the sand:*

27. *And the rain descended, and the floods came, and the winds blew, and beat upon that house and it fell: and great was the fall of it.*

1 Cor. 9:27. *But I (Paul) keep under my body, and bring it under subjection: lest by any means, when I have preached to others, I myself should be a castaway.*

Castaway, n.

1. One who, or that which, is cast away or shipwrecked.

2. One who is ruined; one who has made moral shipwreck; a reprobate.

Lest…when I have preached to others, I myself should be a castaway. 1 Cor. 9:27.[1]

Even Paul, who wrote most of the New Testament, kept close watch over himself lest he be hardened to sin in the flesh and then not repent.

Heb. 3:12. *Take heed, brethren, lest there be in any of you an evil heart of unbelief, in departing from the living God.*

13. *But exhort one another daily, while it is called today, lest any of you be hardened through the deceitfulness of sin.*

14. *For we are made partakers of Christ, if we hold the beginning of our confidence steadfast to the end.*

There is Power in the Tongue

We need to separate ourselves verbally from who we were in Adam: disobedient sinners. Oh yes, you can keep calling yourself a sinner and continue to be just that; but it's not what God would have for you. He calls you righteous, and He wants you to be in agreement with Him and then to call yourself righteous, because that was His gift to you. Meditate on those words and actually be in that right standing with Him that He says you are. Don't even call yourself a sinner, because doing so is a denial of what Jesus has accomplished for you in His death, burial and resurrection – it's like speaking a curse over yourself. We are the righteousness of God in Christ.

Proverbs. 18:21. *Death and life are in the power of the tongue, and they that love it shall eat the fruit thereof* (whether good or evil).

[1] Webster's English Dictionary, Biblesoft Software.

Rom. 4:17. *...even God, who quickens the dead, and calls those things which be not as though they were.*

God's words create whatever He says, where previously there was nothing; and we are made like Him in that respect: our words also create, whether good or evil depends entirely upon you. So guard your tongue well.

The words we speak can either bless or curse: for ourselves and for others. With inanimate objects, the words we speak are neither right or wrong morally. We can have dominion over the weather, or the wind and waves, in Jesus' name, and it's simply a matter of speaking what we need or warding off adverse effects. Our dominion over such things can be quite limited for other people or on someone else's property, because they have full rights over their property, and they can speak disaster for themselves all day long, not realizing what they are doing. However, if you are performing work on their property, your words can't prevent what they believe and say will happen, but your words will keep "your project" from adverse effects caused by something such as a sudden storm – if you believe.

Mark 11:23. *For verily I say unto you, that whosoever shall say unto this mountain, be thou removed and be cast into the sea, and shall not doubt in his heart, but shall believe that those things he says will come to pass, he shall have whatsoever he says.*

2 Pet. 1:3-4. *3. According as his Divine power hath given unto us all things that pertain unto life and godliness through the knowledge of him that hath called us to glory and virtue.*

4. Whereby are given unto us <u>exceeding great and precious promises</u>: that by these ye might be partakers of the Divine nature, having escaped the corruption that is in the world through lust.

2 Co. 1:20. *For all of the promises of God in him are yes and in him Amen, unto the glory of God by us.*

All of God's promises to us are "yes" from Him, and we give the "Amen" (so be it). How do we receive His promises? Just like we received salvation: we believe in our heart that God's word on the matter is true (just because He said so), and then we confess or declare it to be ours with our mouth, standing on that promise in faith (that's the hard part: to be continually expecting, knowing we have received). This is how we partake of His Divine nature: we take those promises as our own. He will deny us no beneficial thing (Ps. 34:10 Amp.), because His Word is His will. Ask and receive that your joy may be full (John 16:24). In the example of prayer given by Jesus, He said, *"…Your will be done on earth as it is in heaven"* (Mat 6:10 NKJV), so He's saying that whatever is in heaven is how God wills it to be on earth. So there is no sickness or disease in heaven, so it must be His will that there be no sickness and disease on earth. He wants everyone to believe and be healed, without exception. All things are possible if you only believe (Mat. 9:23). He also gave Spiritual Gifts to the church that are meant to be for the benefit of all: "Miracles," and "Gifts of Healings," which were meant for those who were not matured in their own faith, but yet needed healing (1 Cor. 12:28). Unfortunately, in most churches, there are no spiritual gifts operating, not because the Holy Spirit isn't giving them, but because most people believe the lie that it all disappeared with the Apostles.

So if He gave precious promises to me by which I partake of His nature, and those promises are everywhere in His Word, then suppose I am sick, and I stand on 1 Peter 2:24, which tells me: *Who his own self bare our sins in his own body on the tree, that we being dead to sins, should live unto righteousness, by whose stripes we were healed.* That Word is telling me straight out that I was healed two thousand years ago when Jesus received those stripes for me. So in turn, I have a right to stand on that promise and say, "By Jesus' stripes I was healed: that means I am healed right this moment, in Jesus' name and by His Word." I don't have to ask for it, because it was already provided for me in God's word. I simply give thanks for it. I receive that healing <u>in my spirit</u> the moment I say it, because faith is "now" (if it's in the future, then it's just "hope" and not faith, in which case I receive nothing). I know by His Word that I am healed right now, even if I don't have sensory proof to back it up. An example of faith in prayer is Mark 11:24, which says: *Therefore I say unto you, whatsoever things you desire, when you pray, believe that you receive them, and you shall have them.* You receive in your spirit the moment you pray, and then there can be a time frame before you actually have it or see it with your eyes. The grace God gives us enables us to endure in faith until we actually see the results with our eyes. There would be no need for faith if you saw it right away, and God does require you to have faith. God has ordained that: *the just should live by faith* (Rom 1:17, Gal. 3:11, Heb. 10:38). Faith is required, and faith always says: "I have it" before I ever see it. *So then faith cometh by hearing, and hearing by the word of God* (Rom. 10:17). If you rarely hear or read the Word of God, you will have very little faith operating in your life.

Now there are those who hate the very idea of God healing people. They say that Peter in that verse was talking about spiritual healing, not physical. Well, we think not. When Jesus died for us, His death restored everything that sin took from us: Before sin entered into this world, there was no sickness or disease, no pain, no death, no lack of any kind, no loss of dominion over the Earth, no bondage to Satan. Jesus' death on the cross took all that bondage away. That word "healed" in 1 Peter 2:24 is referring back to Isaiah 53:5 "…and with his stripes we are healed." That word "healed" in the Hebrew meant: to mend (by stitching) i. e., (figuratively), to cure[2]. Obviously, that can't refer to being healed spiritually, because you can't be mended spiritually. Your spirit had to be totally "re-created" within you, made brand new, not healed. In that verse He was talking about being healed of every sickness and disease and all of our pains, and that healing can be yours if you only believe and hold on in faith until it manifests. Accept His Word as truth, and then act like you have received it, because your faith says that you did receive it. Then it must take place because the Father always keeps His Word! You

---

[2] OT 7495 (Strong's, Biblesoft software)

aren't creating something out of nothing by the power of your mind. You are receiving something by faith that the Father has already provided for you in heavenly places (Eph. 1:3). You receive that provision in your spirit and then it manifests in the natural realm. God is a spirit, and whatever you receive from Him comes spiritually. Everything in this physical realm is subject to change by the spiritual, and everything that comes from God requires faith.

The Spirit or The Flesh

Rom. 8:1. *There is therefore no condemnation to them which are in Christ Jesus, who walk not after the flesh, but after the Spirit.*

5. For they that are after the flesh do mind the things of the flesh. But they that are after the Spirit do the things of the Spirit.

6. For to be carnally minded is death; but to be spiritually minded is life and peace.

8. So then they that are in the flesh cannot please God.

9. But ye are not in the flesh, but in the spirit, if so be that the Spirit of God dwell in You. Now if any man has not the Spirit of Christ, he is none of his.

Rom 8:9 Amplified. *But you are not living the life of the flesh, you are living the life of the Spirit, if the (Holy) Spirit of God (really) dwells within you (<u>directs and controls you</u>). But if anyone does not possess the (Holy) Spirit of Christ, he is none of his (he doesn't belong to Christ, is not truly a child of God).*

So…there is now no condemnation to those who are in Christ, who walk not after the flesh but after the Spirit. Obviously, "who walk not after the flesh" is the key issue to being free from condemnation. We cannot be free of condemnation (judgment) if we are walking after the flesh. What does that mean? To walk after the flesh is to mind the things of the flesh, to be carnally-minded. But we just read that to be carnally-minded is death, so that they that are in the flesh cannot please God. What we are speaking of here then is compromise with the world (the flesh) in varying degrees. The spirit of man cannot sin, so it's the soul and its tie with the flesh that presents a problem: the outward man.

Rev. 7:13. *And one of the Elders answered, saying unto me, what are these which are arrayed in white robes? And whence came they?*

And I said unto him, "Sir, thou know." And he said unto me, "These are they which came out of the great tribulation and have washed their robes (long, flowing outer garments) *and have made them white in the blood of the lamb."*

Jude 1:22. *And of some having compassion, making a difference.*

23. *And others save with fear, pulling them out of the fire, hating even the garment spotted by the flesh.*

This verifies that it's the outer garment or robe, the soul linked with the flesh that interferes with walking after the Spirit.

In Revelation 2-3 Jesus speaks to the seven types of churches that will be present at the time of the seven years of Revelation. Of those, six churches have varying degrees of compromise with the world: One church was denounced as being dead even though "they" thought they were alive; one church enters that time already enduring persecution (being tested); another church had lost their first love for Christ and had grown cold, needing to become "hot" again for the Lord; another church was lukewarm and would be spewed out of His mouth if they didn't change; and one church, the church of Philadelphia, is given an open door that no one can close, because they had a little strength, have kept His word, and have not denied His name. Because they have kept the word of His patience (His patient endurance), He will keep them from the hour of temp-tation (testing).

It's a sad thing that six of seven churches are not living the Word as God desires and will end up facing a horrendous time of testing without the hedge of protection that God normally provides for them, and it's coming up soon. If one church is provided protection, and the other six are not because they are living after the flesh, then that is condemnation (judgment) upon those churches, and it verifies that "living not after the flesh" is the requirement for living free from condemnation. What He means by living after the flesh here is a practice of sin, being attuned to the world's mores, accepting them and incorporating them into our lives, and thinking it's all okay. With God it's not okay at all.

Grafted In, Grafted Out

Rom. 11:16. *For if the first fruit be Holy, the lump is also Holy; and if the root be Holy, so are the branches.*

And if some of the branches be broken off, and thou being a wild olive tree, were grafted in among them and with them partake of the root (Jesus) *and fatness of the olive tree.*

Rom. 11:20. *Well because of unbelief they were broken off* (grafted out), *and thou stand by faith. Be not high-minded, but fear:* (This is warning #1)

21. For if God spared not the natural branches (Israel), *take heed lest he spare not thee.* (This is warning #2)

22. Behold therefore the goodness and severity of God: on them which fell, severity: but toward thee, goodness, <u>if thou continue in his goodness</u>: otherwise thou also shall be cut off. (This is warning #3)

23. And they also, if they abide not still in unbelief, shall be grafted in: for God is able to graft them in again.

That seems very plain. God meant what He said and said what He meant. It's unusual to have three warnings given out like that in a row, however, and it tends to make a person stop and think. Obviously God wanted to make a point. He never takes away our free will, and He absolutely despises unbelief; we just hadn't realized how much. God wants His Word to be believed, exactly as He says it, without reservation, and it's those who stand on that Word, believing and expecting, who come out on the other side: healed, strengthened, delivered, prospering, and whole, completely at one with Him.

Enter Into Rest

Heb. 4:9. *There remains therefore a rest to the people of God.*

10. For he that is entered into his rest, he also hath ceased from his own works, as God did from His.

11. Let us labor therefore to enter into that rest, lest any man fall after the same example of unbelief.

God is not talking about physical rest. The Pharisees were constantly taking what Jesus said and relating it to the law and the physical realm, when in reality, He really meant those things to be in the spiritual. This is a spiritual rest, which is a seventh day of creation rest. Those born of God are remembering to keep the Lord's Day holy – every day, because every day is of the Lord in that spiritual day of rest. They cease from their own work, because now they live after the Spirit and do those works, which God has ordained for them from before the foundation of the world.

Heb. 3:13. *But exhort one another daily, while it is called today.*

Heb 3:15. *While it is said, today, if ye will hear his voice, harden not your hearts* (through unbelief), *as in the day of provocation.*

God doesn't say, "Get right with me while it's Sunday." Today is a time that is not restricted to any day of the week.

Heb 4:4. *For he spoke in a certain place of the seventh day on this wise, and God did rest the seventh day from all his works.*

Heb. 4:3. *For we which have believed do enter into rest, as he said, as I have sworn in my wrath, if they shall enter into my rest: although the works were finished from the foundation of the world.*

We are in God's seventh day rest by our faith: we believed and entered into God's rest.

Col. 2:14. *Blotting out the handwriting of ordinances that was against us, which was contrary to us, and took it out of the way, nailing it to the cross.*

15. And having spoiled principalities and powers, he made a show of them in it, triumphing over them in it.

16. Let no man therefore judge you in meat or drink, or in respect of a holiday, or of a new moon, or of the Sabbath days.

Because we believe, we are in God's rest every single day, and every day is holy, as we follow the leading of the Holy Spirit and walk not after the flesh. We have ceased from all of our works and walk after the Spirit. We are not profitable servants: We only do what the Spirit of God directs us to do (Luke 17:10). It's His work, not ours, and it's done under His power; and we do what He prompts us to do.

Living In Faith

These are some of the things we believe about living in faith:

Jude 1:18 NKJV. *How that they told you that there would be mockers in the last time, who would walk according to their own ungodly lusts.*

19. *These are sensual persons, who cause divisions, not having the Sprit.*

But you, beloved, <u>building yourselves up on your most Holy Faith, praying in the Holy Spirit.</u>

Praying in the Holy Spirit builds up your faith! What a great thing that is, but it's not possible to pray in the Holy Spirit (tongues) if you have not been baptized with the Holy Spirit. The Holy Spirit baptizes us in Jesus when we are saved; but Jesus baptizes us with the Holy Spirit and with fire in the Baptism of the Holy Spirit (Matt. 3:11, NKJV; Luke 3:16, NKJV). In John 20:22 (NKJV), Jesus appeared to the disciples in the upper room and "...*He breathed on them and said to them, 'Receive the Holy Spirit.'*" Then later in Acts 1:4 (NKJV), *And being assembled together with* them, *he* (Jesus) *commanded them not to depart from Jerusalem, but to wait for the promise of the Father, which,* He said, *"you have heard from me, for John truly baptized with water, but you will be baptized with the Holy Spirit not many days from now."* In the upper room experience, when He breathed on them, they received the salvation experience; but in Acts, after appearing to them throughout the forty days after His death, He told them they would be baptized in the Holy Spirit not many days from now. That baptism was a totally different experience: In it they received "power" to operate in the kingdom. Without that baptism, there is no power, and being without power is like trying to wage war with little or no weapons to fight with, and that never works. But again, no one is making you operate in the things of God. It's your choice always.

Acts 2:39 NKJV. *For the promise is unto you, and to your children, and to all that are afar off, even as many as the Lord our God shall call.* (Nothing died off with the Apostles.)

1 John 2:27 NKJV. *But the anointing which you have received of him abides in you, and you do not need that anyone teach you, but as the same anointing teaches you concerning all things, and is true, and is not a lie, and just as it has taught you, you will abide in him.*

Rom. 8:24 NKJV. *For we are saved in this hope: but hope that is seen is not hope: for why does one still hope for what he sees?*

25. But if we hope for what we do not see, we eagerly wait for it with perseverance.

Biblical hope is a confident expectation in a person or thing. *Now faith is the substance of things hoped for, the evidence of things not seen* (Heb. 11:1). Our faith gives substance (reality) to the hope we have, the surety for it. Our faith stamps it "done."

When we pray in the Spirit (tongues), the Holy Spirit prays for the will of the Father in our lives, which is wonderful, because at times we really haven't a clue about what or how we should pray. He prays the Word of God that's needed for our situation to the Father, and we are sure of receiving it.

Rom 8:27 NKJV. *And he that searches the hearts knows what is the mind of the Spirit, because he makes intercession for the saints according to the will of God.*

You know, God can use you through that speaking in the Spirit to have an effect upon the whole world, because it allows the Holy Spirit to pray through you for anything that God desires to have happen in this world to benefit His saints. Who knows what mighty things happen because you cooperate with Him in that way. It's so powerful. Why do you think Paul told the Corinthian church, *I thank my God, I speak with tongues more than ye all* (1 Cor. 14:18).

Rom 8:26 NKJV. *Likewise the Spirit also helps in our weaknesses* (inability to perform): *for we do not know what we should pray for as we ought, but the Spirit Himself makes intercession for us with groanings which cannot be uttered* (articulated in our natural language).

The Holy Spirit lives inside of us, in our spirit, and He helps us tremendously in everything we do. He helps us come to the place in which God wants us to be. We ask everything in Jesus' name, believing we receive it. We declare in Jesus' name that we have what we ask for, and we wait patiently for it. This process helps us to trust God in an unwavering, absolute faith, because if we do not waiver, He always comes through (James 1:6). Living one day at a time, we never worry, believing and knowing that God's Word can't let us down. His grace is sufficient for today, and tomorrow we will have new provision, new grace to see us through. His mercies are new every morning (Lam 22-23).

We have the truth of God's Word when what we say satisfies all of the contradictions to our viewpoint, not just some of them. When we worship the Lord God our Father with all that is within us, and then seek first the Kingdom of God and his righteousness, everything else will fall into place in our lives. He is the priority, not our wives or husbands, or children, or jobs, or money, or homes, or properties: we are just stewards of those things. We have to be willing to give up everything we are or have, rather than to reject him, up to and including our very life. He is the All Powerful, All Knowing, All Present, All Loving, and Wonderful God. Praise be His Name!

Our hope is that you will check out everything that is written here. Do not say that you see without checking first, because that can cause unbelief and blindness (John 9:39-41). What really matters in this life is the relationship we have with the Father through Jesus, and in that relationship, the Holy Spirit, who was sent by the Father to be our comforter and advocate, will teach us all things and bring us into ever increasing levels of glory as we become more like Christ.

Jude 25. *To the only wise God our Savior, be glory and majesty, dominion and power, both now and forever. Amen.*

As an aside, have you ever thought about the Lord returning for His church and what that entails? He is returning for a complete bride, a complete church, without spot or blemish. Because it is complete, it includes all of those six churches that are fated to go through the hour of testing. You will be here, even if you are part of the Philadelphia church, a church that does everything right, because He's not returning for just one portion of the "bride," but for the whole, complete bride.

The Greek words, *"tereso ek,"* meaning "keep from," relating to the hour of temptation (testing) in Rev. 3:10, are an interesting combination: "To keep" (*tereo*) means to watch over with the eye, to keep from loss or harm[3]. Okay, does that sound like you are somewhere out of danger? If you were taken to be with the Lord in heaven, He would not have to keep close watch over you in a protective mode; and there's nothing that could harm you in heaven. Obviously, then, you are not in heaven just yet. You are here with the other churches, except that you have a hedge of protection around you.

The word: "from" (*ek*) means to be pulled out from within[4]. It's only used in that combination with the verb "to keep" (*tereo*) one other time: John 17:15 (NKJV). *I do not pray that you should take them out of the world, but that you should keep them from the evil one.* That "keep from" was Jesus' prayer for his apostles and disciples, and for all of His people up until the time He returns. It was a hedge of protection for them in order to spread the Gospel throughout the whole Earth. Scripture always interprets scripture. If for the apostles and disciples up to this present time, it meant that He would watch over them with His eye and keep them from loss or harm. Why on Earth would it mean to utterly remove the Philadelphia church entirely from the scene before anything hazardous happens? He didn't do that for the apostles, so why would He do that for us? If Scripture interprets Scripture, that certainly isn't going to happen. We will be here, and

---

[3] NT 5083 (Strong's, Biblesoft Software)

[4] NT 1537 (Exegetical Dictionary of NT, Biblesoft Software)

we will be protected through the midst of it (the time of testing) if we are a part of that Philadelphia church. However, if we are fooling ourselves and are not part of that church, then we are facing some truly hard times indeed.

The truth is that it's a matter of legal rights again. God has to have a physical presence (His people) on this Earth to retain ownership of the Earth. When Adam defected and Satan stole the dominion of the Earth from him, God needed to make a covenant with Abraham in order to establish a legal right here on Earth to send Jesus, His Son, to be born of a woman and to die for the sins of mankind; but what a man of faith Abraham proved to be! He took God at His word, and knowing that Isaac, his son, was the son of promise from which all his offspring were to come, he still obeyed God's request to offer him up as a sacrifice. On their way there, Isaac asked his father where the animal of sacrifice was. Abraham answered that God would provide it. He believed that, no matter how things looked, Isaac would still be the son of promise, even if God had to raise him from the dead. Of course, everyone knows the outcome: God prevented Abraham from completing the sacrifice at the last moment. So what right did God have to ask such a thing? Well, at that time, a blood covenant gave both parties the right to call upon the other for anything that they needed that the other person possessed, even a life if it was needed. If Abraham had refused to offer Isaac, God would have had no legal right to send His only son, Jesus, to be born as a man and offer Himself as a sacrifice for all men, paying the debt of sin.

God's kingdom was then established through Jesus in his people: those who accept Him as Lord and Savior. If His people leave, God's legal rights end entirely because his kingdom leaves. It becomes Satan's world by default. That means that God's people must remain here until the kingdom can be passed on to the woman, faithful Israel.

What's taking place is simple really: Adam's lease is running out, and to stay here as the "little god" of this world, Satan and his Anti-Christ have to either destroy all of believing Israel so that there is no one left to receive God's kingdom when the church is pulled out. At that point God's kingdom ends. Or he must kill off every Christian on the Earth so that God's kingdom cannot be passed on to the faithful woman, Israel, and then God's kingdom also ends.

One of Anti-Christ's acts after he takes power at the midpoint of the seven-year Tribulation period is to attempt to destroy the faithful woman (Israel) who is hidden away in the wilderness, but the attempt is thwarted by God's protection. When that fails, he persecutes…*the rest of her seed* (Christians), *which keep the commandments of God, and have the testimony of Jesus Christ* (Rev 14:17).

Believe it or not, he almost carries out his plan, except that Jesus tells us that the time of persecution is cut short or no flesh would be saved: Matt. 24:22. *And except those days shall be shortened, there should no flesh be saved: but for the elect's sake those days shall be shortened,* (not the time of Anti-Christ's reign, but the time of testing).

It's interesting that Jesus says in Luke 18:8, "…*Nevertheless, when the Son of Man cometh, shall he find faith on the Earth?"* He wouldn't have said that if it weren't a possibility. In this He wasn't talking about finding his people alive because the Father cuts short the time of persecution in order to save them, but He was pondering whether or not His people would hold on to their "faith" in Him. That's why it's critical for all of God's people to patiently endure "in faith" and not be tricked or deceived throughout that time, thereby allowing themselves to be eliminated physically or spiritually. That's why Jesus emphatically told us in Matthew 24:23-26. 23. *Then if any man say unto you, "Lo, here is Christ, or there;" <u>believe it not.</u>*

24. *For there shall arise false Christs, and false prophets, and shall show great signs and wonders; in so much that, if it were possible, they would deceive the very elect.*

25. *Behold, I have told you before.*

26. *Wherefore, if they shall say to you, "Behold, he is in the desert; <u>go not forth</u>: behold, he is in the secret chambers, <u>believe it not.</u>"*

27. *For as lightening comes out of the east and shineth unto the west, so shall also the coming of the Son of Man be.*

We can't let the enemy deceive us into coming out from where the Lord is protecting us, thereby destroying us before our time. We must patiently endure until the Lord returns.

In order to have an "hour of testing" spoken of in Revelation, God the Father must lift the hedge of protection from his people, and indeed He does: Rev.13:7. *And it was given unto him to make war with the saints, and to overcome them: and power was given him over all kindreds, and tongues, and nations.* He (the beast, the Anti-Christ) couldn't make war with the saints and overcome them if God didn't lift His hedge of protection from them. Here's the interesting part of all this, however: The Father lifts the hedge of protection spoken of by Jesus before He died, "*…protect them from the evil one.*" So now, because the church of Philadelphia merits protection throughout the Anti-Christ's reign, The Father installs a new protection having a different wording:

Rev 3:10. *Because thou hast kept the word of my patience, I also will keep thee from the hour of temptation* (testing), *which shall come upon all the world, to try them who dwell upon the Earth.*

That protection is: "Keep thee from the hour of temptation;" and the "hour of temptation" is defined by Revelation 13:7 " *…it was given unto him to make war on the saints and to overcome them.* So God's protection is that the Anti-Christ will not be able to make war on them and overcome them if they are the church of Philadelphia. That's huge! That's incredible protection, and the people of that church will carry on as they always have: They will bind the powers of the enemy; they will speak the word with boldness and with power; they will do exploits and confound the enemy at every turn. They will witness to the world around them and perform miracles, signs, and wonders in Jesus' name. And then when they have patiently endured through that time, the Lord will return, his return taking place just prior (Mat

24:37-42; Luke 17:27-36) to the beginning of God's wrath, the trumpet judgments and bowl judgments of Revelation, sometime within the last three-and-a-half years of Revelation.